Piano • Vocal • Guitar

Disney's

TARZAN

CONTENTS

Two Worlds 4

Two Worlds (Reprise) 12

You'll Be in My Heart 15

Son of Man 20

Trashin' the Camp 29

Strangers Like Me 38

Two Worlds (Finale) 44

You'll Be in My Heart (Pop Version) 48

Trashin' the Camp (Pop Version) 57

ISBN 0-634-00161-2

Walt Disney Music Company

DISTRIBUTED BY

HAL•LEONARD®
CORPORATION
7777 W. BLUEMOUND RD. P.O. BOX 13213 MILWAUKEE, WI 53213

Two Worlds

Words and Music by
PHIL COLLINS

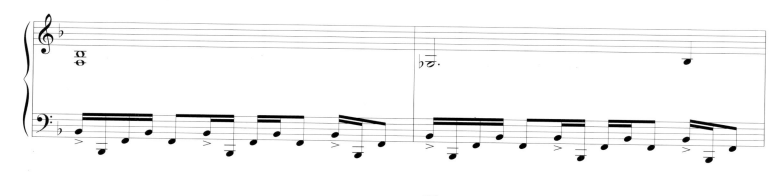

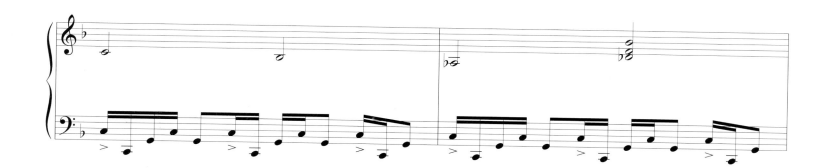

You'll Be in My Heart

Words and Music by
PHIL COLLINS

Trashin' the Camp

Words and Music by
PHIL COLLINS

N.C.

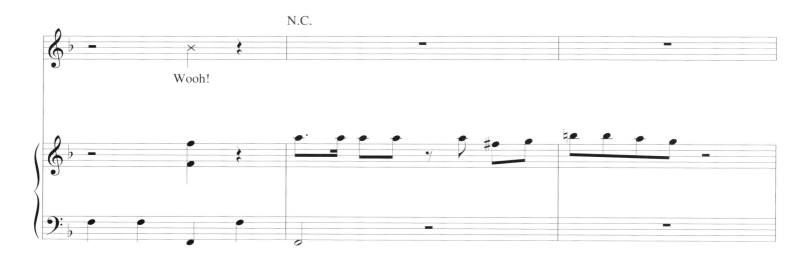

Wooh!

Shoo-bee - doo   dab - bee - dah   n'doo-bee - doo   n'da - bee   dah-dah'n - doo ___ dah.

8vb throughout

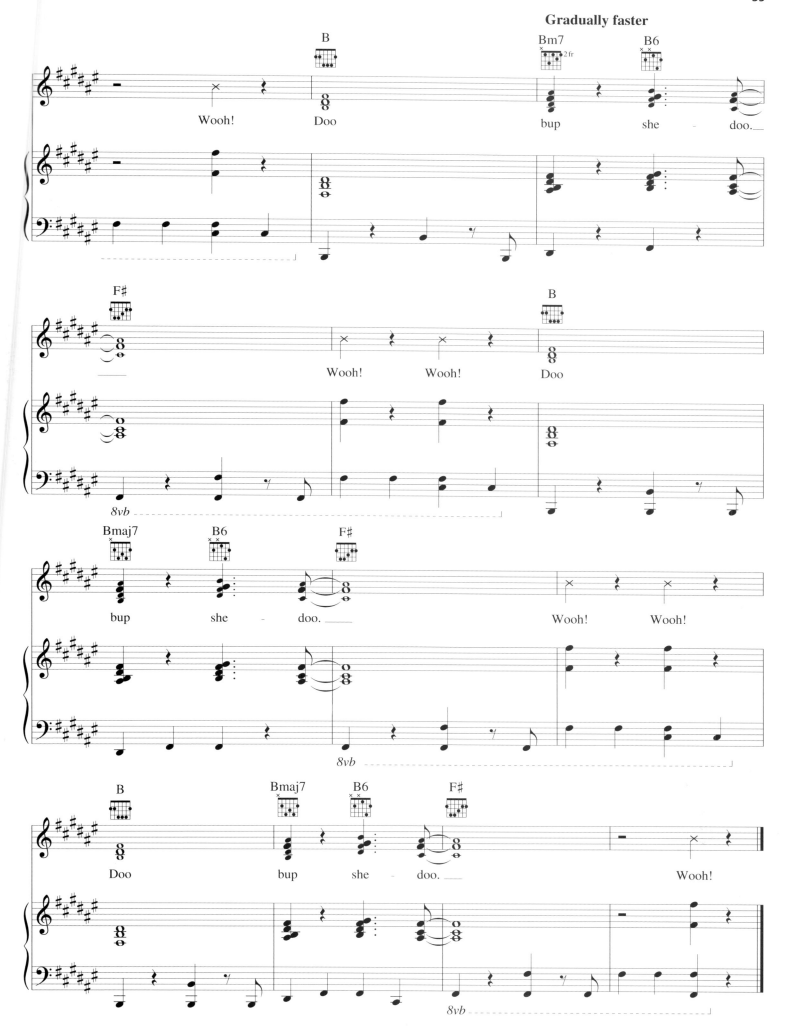

Strangers Like Me

Words and Music by
PHIL COLLINS

You'll Be in My Heart
(Pop Version)

Words and Music by
PHIL COLLINS

Moderately

Come stop your cry-ing; it will be all right.

Just take my hand, hold it tight. _____ I will pro-tect you from

all a-round _ you. I will be here; don't you _ cry.

Trashin' the Camp
(Pop Version)

Words and Music by
PHIL COLLINS

Moderately in 2

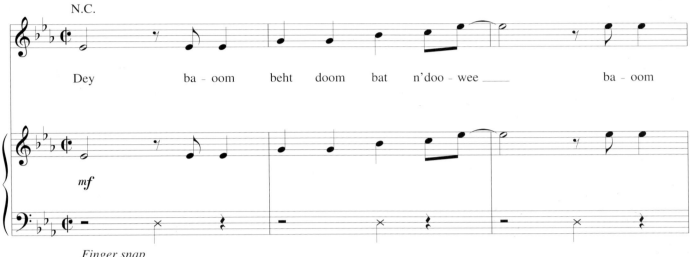

Dey ba - oom beht doom bat n'doo - wee ___ ba - oom

Finger snap

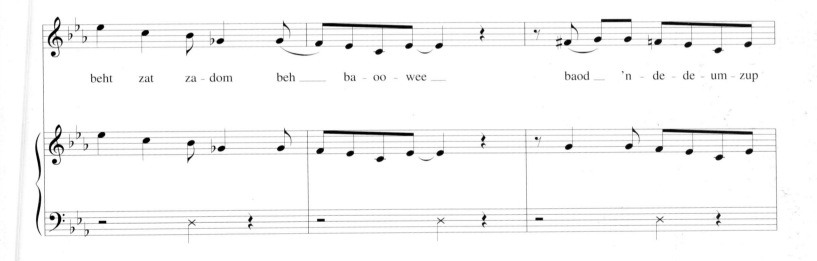

beht zat za - dom beh ___ ba - oo - wee ___ baod ___ 'n - de - de - um - zup

zep zep zep zeh ___ dap za. Za - be - dap zoo - be -

58

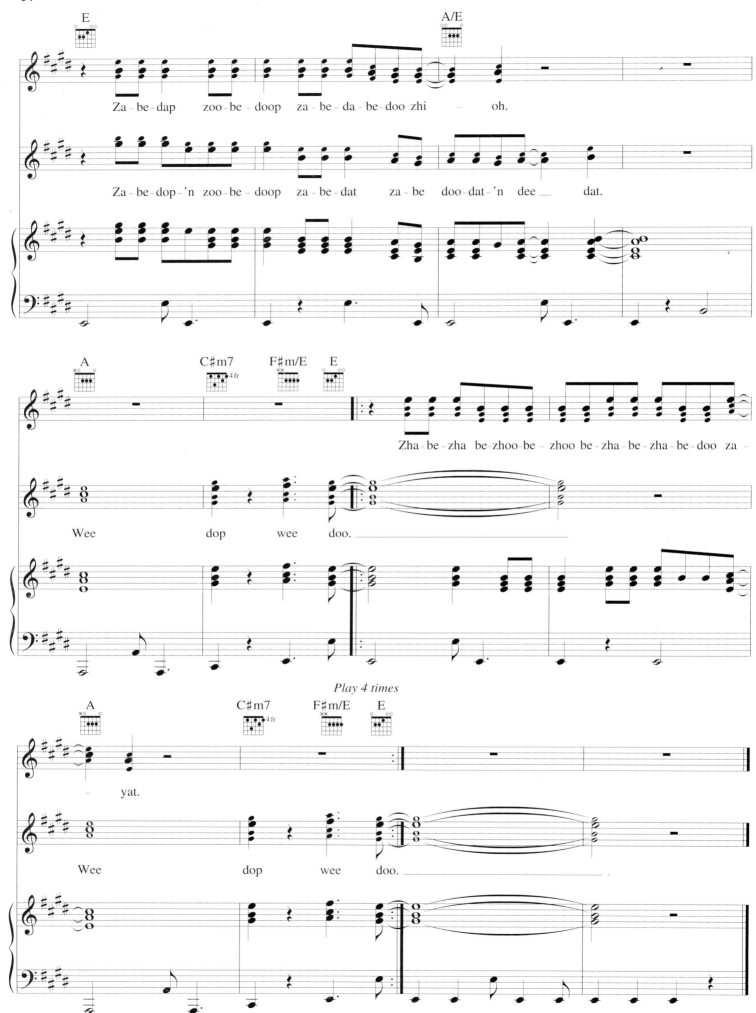